THE BEE

Friend of the Flowers

Text and photos by
Paul Starosta

French series editor, Valérie Tracqui

Charlesbridge

© 2005 by Charlesbridge Publishing. Translated by Elizabeth Uhlig.

© 2002 by Editions Milan under the title *L'Abeille*
300 rue Léon-Joulin, 31101 Toulouse Cedex 100, France
www.editionsmilan.com
French series editor, Valérie Tracqui

Published by Charlesbridge
85 Main Street
Watertown, MA 02472
(617) 926-0329
www.charlesbridge.com

Library of Congress Cataloging-in-Publication Data
Starosta, Paul.
  [Abeille. English]
  The bee : friend of the flowers / Paul Starosta ; [translated by
Elizabeth Uhlig].
    p. cm.
  ISBN 1-57091-629-2 (softcover)
1. Honeybee—Juvenile literature. I. Title.
QL568.A6S76713 2005
595.79'9—dc22   2004018934

Printed in China
(sc) 10 9 8 7 6 5 4 3 2 1

PHOTO CREDITS
All photos are by Paul Starosta.

AMONG THE FLOWERS

In springtime nature wakes from a winter sleep. The air is sweet and fragrant as flowers bloom. The bright colors of the meadow flowers attract many buzzing insects.

A honeybee flutters around her hive, making sure that she will be able to find her way back. Then she flies into the field, searching for flowers. Among all these colors and scents, the honeybee chooses a flower that has a lot of nectar. Nectar is a sweet liquid made by flowers to attract bees and other pollinators.

Honeybees can't see the color red, but they can see these poppies using their ultraviolet vision.

This is the same photo from pages 4–5, as seen under ultraviolet light.

A honeybee returns
to a flower that is
rich in nectar.

THE POLLEN BASKET

All worker bees are female. One of their many jobs is to gather food from flowers. Thanks to their long tongue, honeybees can soak up nectar that is inside a flower. They store nectar in a sac called a honey stomach. They must visit about 100 flowers to fill their honey stomach. Honeybees also gather pollen. A honeybee uses her jaws to grasp the stamens of the flower, then shakes the stamens, covering herself in pollen. A stamen is the male part of the flower, and it makes pollen.

Spiders prey on honeybees, attacking when one lands on a flower.

A honeybee lands on a flower and soaks up nectar with her long, hairy tongue.

After leaving a flower, a honeybee cleans herself with the brushes on her hind feet. She moves the pollen into pollen baskets, which are hollows on her rear legs. Once her pollen baskets are full or her honey stomach is filled with nectar, the honeybee goes back to her hive.

This honeybee's pollen basket is full of orange pollen from a dandelion.

THE BEE'S DANCE

Once a honeybee nears the hive, guard bees greet her. These are worker bees that protect the hive and make sure that the honeybee belongs to their colony. The way is finally clear, and the honeybee enters.

Inside the dark hive, thousands of honeybees make buzzing sounds with their wings. The honeybee gatherer touches one of them and offers a bit of nectar that she has regurgitated (spit up) from her honey stomach. After many nectar exchanges, the honeybee begins to dance. This dance shows the other bees the way to the flowers she has found.

Honeybees return to their hive before the sun sets.

A man-made hive contains thousands of bees.

Each bee that wants to enter the hive must first get past the worker bees that are on guard duty.

These honeybees are exchanging nectar.

The bees form a circle around the gatherer. They touch her with their antennae to feel which way she moves. The gatherer wags her abdomen while moving a few steps in a straight line to show the direction of the flowers. The faster she wags, the closer the flowers are to the hive. Once the other honeybees get this message, they fly away to collect more pollen and nectar.

The colony circles a honeybee as she dances.

MAKING HONEY

The worker bees that have stayed behind in the hive exchange nectar mouth-to-mouth. Each honeybee transforms a little of the nectar from her honey stomach into a food, called honey. The inside of the hive has thousands of small wax cells that make up the honeycomb. Each worker bee will deposit some honey into one of these cells. Pollen, an important source of protein for honeybees, is stored in separate wax cells to be used later for food.

A long tongue helps honeybees to suck in the nectar that is hidden at the base of flowers, as well as to deposit honey in the cells of the honeycomb.

Each flower's pollen has its own color. This cross section of the honeycomb shows that the honeybees have visited three different kinds of flowers.

When they return to the hive, gatherers unload their pollen balls into the honeycomb to share with the others. The rest of the worker bees pile up the pollen balls in the cells.

A worker bee fans her wings for hours on end in order to thicken the honey.

The honey is still too thin to be stored. The excess water needs to evaporate. Sitting above the honeycomb, worker bees fan their wings to create a current of air. It's hard work, but efficient. Soon the hive cools off and the honey thickens. Fanning changes the temperature of the hive by a quarter of a degree. A honeybee can measure the temperature with the tips of her antennae.

WAX— A BUILDING MATERIAL

Thanks to the honeybees' fanning, the honey is thick enough for the cells to be closed up with wax. When worker bees are 12 days old, their body is ready to produce wax. They secrete wax through glands in their abdomen. Then they take the wax and use their mouth to shape it into the honeycomb.

A job for each bee

Worker bees are infertile females. Each worker bee's job is determined by her age and the needs of the hive. A worker bee is first a nurse, then a wax worker, then a guard bee, and finally a gatherer. The only fertile female in the hive is the queen. Her job is to mate with drones and then to lay eggs for the rest of her life. Drones are male bees, and their only job is to mate with the queen.

The wax workers in the hive must eat 10 pounds of honey in order to make 1 pound of wax. They work in groups to construct the honeycomb.

This honeybee uses her jaws to spread out each bit of wax.

Unused pollen turns moldy in the open cells of the honeycomb.

THE BROOD NEST

Having mated with the drones, the queen bee's job is to lay eggs to ensure the survival of the colony. In the hive the queen stays in the middle of a small circle of worker bees. From time to time, she gets food from one of her young worker bees, while the others lick her. By doing this the workers swallow chemicals that are then passed mouth-to-mouth as the honeybees exchange food. These chemicals prevent the worker bees from becoming fertile.

Worker bees tend to the brood nest.

At the center of this photo, the queen can be seen laying eggs. The worker bees pile up food supplies around the edges of the brood nest.

The queen bee checks each wax cell to make sure it is empty before she lays an egg in it. Then she continues her tour of the other cells. These cells make up the brood nest. A queen can lay up to 3,000 eggs in one day. These eggs will produce worker bees. Keeping up the population of worker bees is important to the survival of the colony. Fortunately laying eggs is the queen's only task. The younger worker bees are responsible for raising this large family.

When they are laid, the eggs are deposited deep down in the bottom of each cell.

The tireless, egg-laying queen bee is surrounded by worker bees that feed her after about every 20 eggs she lays.

LARVA FOOD

The worker bees keep the temperature inside the brood nest at 95 degrees Fahrenheit. After three days a small, worm-shaped larva emerges from each egg. The nurse bees are ready to give the larvae their first meal of royal jelly. Royal jelly is a secretion made by young worker bees. On the fourth day, larvae are fed beebread, a mixture of water, pollen, and honey. After the larvae have been on this diet for four days, each cell is sealed up with a wax cap. Each larva will go through a metamorphosis, or change, first into a nymph and then into an adult.

Nurse bees are never idle. They have little time to feed each larva the necessary 6,000 times.

Alone in her cell, the larva weaves a silk cocoon. Then she metamorphoses into a nymph.

In 6 days the larvae have grown so much (500 times the weight of the eggs) that they now fill up the cells.

Twenty-one days later, a new worker bee breaks through the wax cap. During her lifetime, which can last five weeks to five months, a worker bee will do several different jobs inside the hive. Worker bees usually don't become gatherers until they are older.

An adult bee leaves her cell by ripping off the wax cap with her jaws.

THE QUEEN LEAVES THE HIVE

After another winter passes and spring returns, drones are born. The drones wait for the new queen to arrive. When the current queen stops laying eggs, some of the worker bees build cells around a group of recently laid eggs. These larvae are fed only royal jelly and will become queen bees.

The current queen knows that one of her daughters will take her place as the new queen. So she flies away, followed by a swarm of worker bees. This swarm of thousands of bees will build a new hive. A new colony has been established.

The queen bee flies away with thousands of worker bees in order to build a new hive.

Drones have a thicker body than worker bees do.

The swarm finds a temporary place to rest. Scouts will find a new location to build a hive and then will dance around the swarm so it knows in which direction to fly.

After arriving in her new home, a gatherer starts collecting nectar and pollen.

THE NEW QUEEN

The colony in the old hive is now orphaned, but not for long. Sixteen days after the new queen's egg was laid, she breaks out of her cell.

The new queen searches the rest of the hive for competitors. If she finds any, she will kill them while they're still in their cell. If any other queens make it out of a cell alive, the two queen bees will fight to the death.

A few days later, the winner will mark the area with her scent. In the days that follow, the new queen joins the drones in flight. Once a drone mates, he dies. The queen mates with many of the drones.

After mating the queen returns to her hive. Her only job is to lay eggs. She will not leave the hive again until the worker bees start to produce a new queen.

The queen larva's cell is open at the bottom, but she doesn't fall out because she is stuck to its ceiling with royal jelly.

The drones gather and wait for the queen.

A queen bee weighs more than twice as much as a worker bee.

WINTER IN THE HIVE

The only purpose a drone has is to mate with the queen. Drones that don't mate with the queen are useless to the colony. The worker bees force the drones out of the hive. The drones try to resist, but without stingers they can't put up much of a fight. When winter comes, these homeless drones will die.

Over 20,000 bees are huddled close together to keep warm.

Even when they're not working, the honeybees need to eat. A hive can make 60 pounds of honey in a season, but it only needs about 30 pounds for the winter.

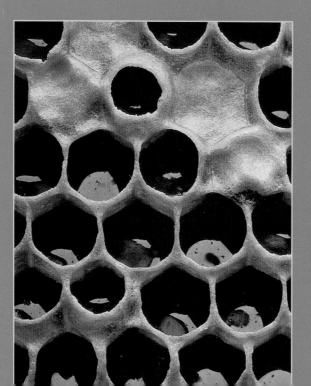

It's too cold to go out in winter. The worker bees stay in the middle of the hive, around their queen. They have stored enough honey for the colony to survive through the winter. The worker bees grow fat in the cold weather, but as soon as spring arrives, they will once again take up their work of visiting the flowers.

22

Snow covers the hive.
The bees will not leave
until springtime.

Many honeybees are domesticated, meaning they are cared for by humans. They are sheltered, tended to, and moved from one hive to another by the beekeeper, who is called an apiarist. Honeybees and silkworms are the only domesticated insects. All bees are also useful because they cross-pollinate flowers, especially those of fruit trees.

HONEY FOR EVERYONE

Honeybees store away more honey than they need to last through the winter. A beekeeper can then remove some of it, about 30 pounds, without endangering the colony. Depending on the kinds of flowers that the honeybees have visited, different types of honey will be produced (clover, orange blossom, alfalfa, etc.).

OTHER BEE PRODUCTS

Wax, pollen, and royal jelly are also harvested. Propolis, or bee glue, is tree resin that the bees use to insulate the hive. It can also be used in medicines. Beekeepers are very careful not to endanger a hive by removing too much of any one product. In the past, an entire colony would be killed with each harvest.

A bee helps
fertilize flowers.

POLLINATION

While collecting nectar from a flower, a honeybee gets covered with pollen. When she rubs against the next flower, some of the pollen falls into it. Now the flower has been fertilized. This is called pollination. Farmers use beehives to pollinate their fruit trees. This helps plants produce fruit.

Varroa mites

Like all living things, honeybees sometimes get sick. Antibiotics or other medicines are successful in treating sick colonies. But for the last few years varroa mites have been attacking hives. New medicines are being developed to cure honeybee colonies.

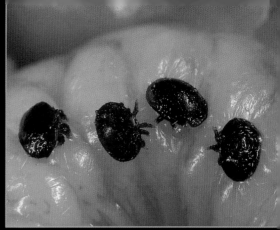

These tiny eight-legged creatures are varroa mites.

Beekeepers keep the bees calm by filling the hive with smoke.

Selecting a species

Each bee species is unique. A beekeeper chooses a species according to his needs and tastes. In general it is better to raise a local species because it is adapted to the region.

Careful, bees sting!

When a bee's stinger pierces another insect's outer shell, it comes out again easily. But small barbs keep the tip of the stinger from coming out of human skin. When a bee stings you, she leaves the stinger and a piece of her internal organs stuck in your skin. This causes her to die. Honeybees only attack to defend their hive. So it's possible to safely observe them if you stay far enough away from the hive.

THE BEE'S COUSINS

Like all insects, a honeybee has six legs. All bees belong to the order Hymenoptera. Wasps, which belong to the same order, are often confused with bees. Both bees and wasps gather nectar to feed their larvae, but unlike bees, wasps are very aggressive and also feed on other insects.

YELLOW JACKETS

Yellow jackets are a type of wasp that is found throughout North America. They build their nests out of paper and feed insects to their larvae. In winter the colony dies, except for a few fertilized females that will each become the queen of a new wasp nest in the spring. Unlike a bee's stinger, a wasp's stinger is smooth at the end. So a yellow jacket can sting a person more than once.

HORNETS

Hornets are the largest wasps. Like yellow jackets, hornets build paper nests and are aggressive when their nest is disturbed. Hornets live in North America, Europe, and Asia.

BUMBLEBEES

Bumblebees live in small colonies of a few hundred bees. While honeybees remain alive through the winter, bumblebees die. The only ones that survive are a few fertilized females. In the spring each female will start laying eggs in her new nest. Bumblebees build nests in mossy places, hollows, and underground burrows. They also pollinate flowers and plants, such as tomatoes, that some other bees can't. They can be found in North America, South America, and Europe.

CARPENTER BEES

Unlike honeybees, carpenter bees live alone. A female makes a nest by burrowing a tunnel into rotten wood. In the middle of the nest, she stores up nectar and pollen, and then lays an egg. After closing up this part of the tunnel with a mixture of saliva and sawdust, she begins the process all over again. When she is done, she has a colony of about seven or eight cells. Carpenter bees are found all over the world.

FOR FURTHER READING ON BEES . . .

Cooper, Jason. *Honeybee* (Life Cycles II Series). Vero Beach, FL: Rourke Publishing, 2003.

Hodge, Deborah. *Bees* (Denver Museum Insect Books series). Toronto: Kids Can Press, 2004.

Loewen, Nancy. *Busy Buzzers: Bees in Your Backyard* (Backyard Bugs series). Minneapolis, MN: Picture Window Books, 2004.

USE THE INTERNET TO FIND OUT MORE ABOUT BEES . . .

Honey.com
—This kid-friendly site offers honeybee facts, trivia, and history. There are also links to other cool honeybee websites.
http://www.honey.com/kids/index.html

Bees
—This site from KidsKonnect.com has loads of links to kid-friendly sites focused on bees.
http://www.kidskonnect.com/Bees/BeesHome.html

Lanakids
—A helpful site that tells kids how to avoid bee stings and what to do in case they are stung.
http://www.lanakids.com/beeware.html

INDEX